Sainsbury's

·RECIPE·LIBRARY·

SUMMER
DESSERTS

Sainsbury's

· RECIPE · LIBRARY ·

SUMMER
DESSERTS

Carole Handslip

CONTENTS

Published exclusively for J Sainsbury plc
Stamford House Stamford Street
London SE1 9LL
by Woodhead-Faulkner Ltd
Fitzwilliam House 32 Trumpington Street
Cambridge CB2 1QY

First published 1986
Printed and bound in Italy by Arnoldo Mondadori Editore

INTRODUCTION

Whether you want to make the simplest fruit salad or an exotic strawberry extravaganza, here you will find plenty of exciting, original and attractive ideas.

Although I have included some elaborate desserts, my own favourites are the simple mixtures of those delicious fresh fruits which are available in such vast variety during the summer months – raspberries, redcurrants, blackcurrants, strawberries, to name but a few. Adding a little liqueur to any fresh fruit dish transforms it into something special. For an attractive finishing touch, use soft fruit leaves and scented herbs to decorate.

Ice creams and sorbets are also very much in demand during the summer. These, too, are easy to prepare, and home-made ices are far superior to the commercial varieties. Any fruit purée, many of the fragrant herb teas and even elderflowers can make wonderful ices and sorbets. A fresh, sharp fruit purée can also be turned into a tangy fruit fool or a creamy mousse in minutes.

I have included smatana in quite a few of the recipes; it adds a luscious creaminess without the high fat content of cream and is therefore much healthier. An alternative is yogurt; the thick Greek yogurt is especially delicious, though it does need stirring well to make it really smooth.

I nearly always try to prepare desserts in advance and leave them in the refrigerator until required, so that a minimum of last-minute attention is involved. However, there is one chapter devoted to hot desserts, and obviously some of these do need to be made at the last minute. They would probably be more suitable to serve to the family, rather than when entertaining.

A well-chosen dessert can make or break a meal. It is important to choose a dessert that complements the main course. After a rich main course, choose a light, slightly sharp fruit dish or a sorbet. To round off a lighter meal, opt for a gâteau or pastry dessert.

You will find recipes appropriate for all occasions in the following pages – and don't hide this book away during the winter! Summer fruits freeze well and most of these desserts can be made out of season, using frozen fruit.

NOTES

Ingredients are given in both metric and imperial measures. Use either set of quantities but not a mixture of both in any one recipe.

All spoon measurements are level:
1 tablespoon = one 15 ml spoon
1 teaspoon = one 5 ml spoon.

Ovens should be preheated to the temperature specified.

Eggs are standard size 3 unless otherwise stated.

Sauce recipes are marked with an asterisk and given in the reference section (pages 78–9). Increase or decrease the basic quantities in proportion to obtain the amount required.

FRUIT DESSERTS

POIRES AUX CASSIS

A popular dessert in Burgundy, where crème de cassis originates. You can poach the pears lightly if you prefer, but I like to use really juicy William pears and serve them as they are. Frozen blackcurrants could be used.

350 g (12 oz) blackcurrants
50 g (2 oz) caster sugar
125 ml (4 fl oz) water

2 tablespoons crème de cassis (optional)
6 William pears

Serves 6
Preparation time: 20 minutes
Cooking time: 10 minutes
Freezing: Recommended for sauce only

1. Place the blackcurrants, sugar and water in a pan and cook gently for about 10 minutes, stirring occasionally, until soft.
2. Purée in a food processor or blender, then sieve to remove the seeds. Leave to cool, then add the crème de cassis, if using.
3. Peel, halve and core the pears; arrange on individual dishes. Spoon over the sauce and serve immediately.

SUMMER FRUIT COMPOTE

250 g (8 oz) mixed blackcurrants and redcurrants
2 tablespoons clear honey
4 tablespoons pure orange juice

1 teaspoon arrowroot
250 g (8 oz) strawberries, quartered
2 tablespoons Grand Marnier

Serves 4
Preparation time: 15 minutes, plus cooling
Cooking time: 10 minutes
Freezing: Not recommended

1. Place the blackcurrants and redcurrants, honey and orange juice in a pan, bring to the boil, then cover and simmer gently for 10 minutes, until softened.
2. Strain the fruit and place in a bowl. Return the syrup to the pan.
3. Blend the arrowroot with a little water until smooth, then stir into the syrup. Bring to the boil, stirring constantly until thickened and clear.
4. Pour over the currants, add the strawberries and Grand Marnier, mix together gently and leave to cool.
5. Turn into a glass serving bowl and chill until required. Serve with Crémets*, yogurt or cream.

CERISES À L'ORANGE

340 g (12 oz) can Morello
    cherries
2 teaspoons arrowroot
grated rind and juice of
    1 orange
3 tablespoons kirsch

6 tablespoons double
    cream
1 egg white
1 tablespoon clear honey
about 40 ratafia biscuits
orange rind shreds (see
    below) to decorate

Serves 4
Preparation time:
30 minutes
Freezing:
Not recommended

1. Drain the cherries, place the juice in a pan and bring to the boil. Blend the arrowroot with the orange juice; add to the syrup, stirring constantly until thickened.
2. Stone the cherries, then add to the syrup with 2 tablespoons of the kirsch. Leave to cool.
3. Meanwhile, mix the remaining kirsch with the orange rind, add to the cream and whip until soft peaks form.
4. Whisk the egg white until stiff, then whisk in the honey. Fold into the orange cream.
5. Break each ratafia into 2 or 3 pieces and arrange in 4 individual glass bowls in alternate layers with the cream and cherries, finishing with a layer of cream.
6. Decorate with orange rind shreds and chill until required.

Orange or lemon rind shreds: Pare the rind thinly, using a potato peeler. Cut into very fine strips, about 3.5 cm (1½ inches) long. Blanch in boiling water for 2 minutes. Drain, rinse in cold water, drain again and pat dry with kitchen paper. Use to decorate desserts.

PINEAPPLE SNOW

1 small pineapple
2 tablespoons kirsch
2 egg whites

2 tablespoons clear honey
frosted leaves (see page 42)
    to decorate

Serves 4–6
Preparation time:
15 minutes
Freezing:
Not recommended

1. Halve the pineapple lengthways, remove the hard central core and scoop out the flesh. Place in a food processor or blender with the kirsch and work until smooth.
2. Whisk the egg whites until stiff, then whisk in the honey.
3. Fold in the pineapple purée, spoon into wine glasses and decorate with frosted leaves. Serve immediately, as the dessert separates on standing.

PÊCHES CARDINALES

One of the quickest and most refreshing summer desserts.
For an equally pleasant change, use Strawberry Sauce*
instead of Melba Sauce.

*150 ml (¹/₄ pint) Melba
  Sauce**
*1 tablespoon framboise
  liqueur or kirsch*

*4 peaches
2 tablespoons flaked
  almonds, toasted*

1. Mix together the melba sauce and liqueur.
2. Dip the peaches in boiling water for about 8 seconds, then remove the skins. Cut in half, remove the stones and arrange on 4 individual plates.
3. Spoon over the sauce and sprinkle with the almonds.

Serves 4
Preparation time:
10 minutes, plus
making sauce
Freezing:
Not recommended

TROPICAL FRUIT JELLY

This delicious jelly can be made with any fruits, but banana
and guava do give it the tropical touch.

*300 ml (½ pint) fruit
    cocktail juice
1 envelope gelatine
411 g (14½ oz) can
    guavas in syrup*

*2 bananas, sliced
2 pears, peeled, quartered,
    cored and sliced*

Serves 4–6
Preparation time:
15 minutes, plus
setting time
Freezing:
Not recommended

1. Place 4 tablespoons of the fruit cocktail juice in a small
pan, sprinkle over the gelatine and leave to soak for
5 minutes. Heat gently until dissolved, then mix with the
remaining juice in a bowl.
2. Drain the guavas and add the syrup to the bowl. Slice
the guavas and add to the bowl with the bananas and pears.
3. Pour into 4 or 6 individual moulds, depending on their
size; alternatively pour into a 900 ml (1½ pint) mould.
Chill for 2 hours, to set.
4. To turn out, dip the mould quickly into hot water and
invert onto a serving plate.

ICED MANGO SOUP

A delightful way to finish off a sunny summer lunch in the
garden. Simple to make, so you don't have to spend too
long in the kitchen away from the sun!

*2 mangoes
150 ml (¼ pint) pure
    orange juice
150 ml (¼ pint) sweet
    white wine*

*4 tablespoons smatana or
    double cream
a little milk (optional)*

Serves 4
Preparation time:
10 minutes
Freezing:
Recommended

1. Cut the mangoes either side of the stone and scoop out
all the flesh. Place in a food processor or blender with the
orange juice and work until smooth.
2. Stir in the wine, then pour into individual soup bowls
and chill until required.
3. Thin the smatana with a little milk if necessary, then
swirl a spoonful of smatana or cream into the centre of
each bowl.

STRAWBERRY CHARTREUSE

A very simple dessert to make, and one that looks magnificent when cut. It also looks good sliced onto individual plates and surrounded with the sauce.

1 mango
1 kiwi fruit, peeled and
   sliced
125 g (4 oz) strawberries,
   halved
1 William pear, peeled and
   chopped

300 ml (½ pint) pure
   orange juice
1 envelope gelatine
2 tablespoons Grand
   Marnier
150 ml (¼ pint)
   Strawberry Sauce*

Serves 6
Preparation time:
30 minutes, plus
making sauce and
setting time
Freezing:
Not recommended

1. Cut the mango either side of the stone. Scoop out and chop all the flesh. Place in a 900 ml (1½ pint) ring mould or 500 g (1 lb) loaf tin with the kiwi fruit, strawberries and pear.
2. Place 150 ml (¼ pint) of the orange juice in a small pan and sprinkle over the gelatine. Leave to soak for 5 minutes, then heat very gently until dissolved.
3. Add the remaining orange juice and the Grand Marnier, pour into the mould or tin and chill for 2 hours, until set.
4. To turn out, dip the mould or tin quickly into hot water, then invert onto a serving plate. Cut into slices, and serve with the strawberry sauce.

CHOCOLATE ORANGE CUPS

200 g (7 oz) plain
* chocolate, broken into*
* pieces*
4 oranges

2 tablespoons Grand
* Marnier*
250 ml (8 fl oz) double
* cream*

1. Place the chocolate in a small bowl over a pan of hot water. Bring the water to the boil, then turn off the heat and leave until the chocolate has melted; be careful not to allow any water to get into the basin. Leave to cool.
2. Spread 2 tablespoons of the chocolate onto grease-proof paper and leave until just set. Cut into squares and then into triangles, using a ruler and sharp knife; set aside.
3. Spoon half of the remaining chocolate into 8 paper cake cases and, using the handle of a teaspoon, spread it over the inside of each case. Leave for about 1 hour to set at room temperature, then cover with a second coat of chocolate. Leave to set.
4. Finely grate the zest of 1 orange, mix with the Grand Marnier, then stir into the cream. Whip until it holds its shape.
5. Remove the paper from the chocolate cases and pipe orange cream into each case. Top with chocolate triangles.
6. Peel the remaining oranges; divide all the oranges into segments, discarding all pith. Arrange the chocolate cups and orange segments on individual plates to serve.

Serves 8
Preparation time:
35 minutes, plus
setting time
Freezing:
Not recommended

STRAWBERRY ROMANOFF

This light, creamy dessert is perfect for warm summer days. It is best served with crisp biscuits.

*142 ml (5 fl oz) carton
    double cream
2 tablespoons Grand
    Marnier
1 egg white
1 tablespoon clear honey*

*150 g (5 oz) smatana
350 g (12 oz) strawberries,
    halved
4 frosted strawberry leaves
    (see page 42) to decorate*

Serves 4
Preparation time:
20 minutes
Freezing:
Not recommended

1. Combine the cream and Grand Marnier, then whip until it holds its shape.
2. Whisk the egg white until stiff, then whisk in the honey. Fold into the cream with the smatana.
3. Set aside a few strawberry halves for decoration. Fold the rest into the cream mixture.
4. Spoon into 4 glass serving dishes and chill until required. Decorate with the reserved strawberries and the frosted leaves.

SPICED APPLE LAYER

Choose tall glasses so that the layers in this delicious dessert are more obvious. The dates may be replaced with other dried fruits if you prefer.

*4 tablespoons pure apple
    juice
500 g (1 lb) dessert apples,
    peeled and sliced
1/2 teaspoon ground
    cinnamon*

*125 g (4 oz) chopped dates
150 g (5.3 oz) carton
    natural set yogurt
4 tablespoons smatana
2 tablespoons flaked
    almonds, toasted*

Serves 4
Preparation time:
10 minutes, plus
cooling
Cooking time:
15–20 minutes
Freezing:
Not recommended

1. Place the apple juice with the apples, cinnamon and dates in a heavy-based pan, cover and cook gently for 15–20 minutes until softened, stirring occasionally. Leave to cool.
2. Mix the yogurt and smatana together until smooth.
3. Place half of the apple mixture in 4 individual glasses and cover with half of the yogurt mixture. Repeat the layers. Chill until required.
4. Sprinkle with the almonds to serve.

PRUNES IN BRANDY

*250 g (8 oz) pitted dried
   prunes
350 ml (12 fl oz) pure
   orange juice*

*2 tablespoons brandy
2 oranges*

1. Place the prunes and orange juice in a pan and leave to soak for 30 minutes. Bring to the boil, then cover and cook for 20 minutes. Add the brandy and leave to cool.
2. Meanwhile, peel the zest from the oranges and use to make orange rind shreds (see page 8). Peel the pith from the oranges, then cut the flesh into segments, discarding all pith, and add to the prunes.
3. Spoon into individual glass dishes, sprinkle with the orange shreds and chill until required.
4. Serve with Greek yogurt or smatana if you wish.

Serves 6
Preparation time:
10 minutes, plus
soaking time
Cooking time:
20 minutes
Freezing:
Not recommended

SUMMER SUNDAES

A variation of summer pudding, served in wine glasses. Ideal to serve at an 'al fresco' meal in the summer.

500 g (1 lb) mixed blackberries, blackcurrants and redcurrants	*2 tablespoons clear honey 250 g (8 oz) strawberries, sliced, or raspberries 8 slices wholemeal bread*

Serves 8
Preparation time:
30 minutes, plus chilling
Cooking time:
10 minutes
Freezing:
Recommended, if made in freezer-proof dishes

1. Place the blackberries, blackcurrants and redcurrants, honey and 2 tablespoons water in a heavy-based pan and cook gently for 10 minutes until tender, stirring occasionally.
2. Add the strawberries or raspberries and leave to cool. Strain, reserving the juice.
3. Cut out 16 circles of bread to fit inside the wine glasses and soak in the reserved juice.
4. Place a third of the fruit in 8 wine glasses and top with a circle of bread. Place another third of the fruit on top and cover with another circle of bread. Top with the remaining fruit. Chill for 30 minutes or until required.
5. Serve with smatana or cream if you wish.

STAR FRUIT SALAD

Star fruit, sometimes called Carambola, should be yellow-ish when ripe. The fluted edges begin to go brown, so are best trimmed away with scissors. If unavailable, kiwi fruit makes an equally good addition to this fruit salad.

425 g (15 oz) can lychees in syrup juice of 1 lime 2 tablespoons Cointreau 2 oranges	*1 small Ogen melon, halved and seeded 3 star fruit 1/2 tablespoon shredded lemon balm*

Serves 6
Preparation time:
20 minutes
Freezing:
Not recommended

1. Place the lychees with their syrup, lime juice and Cointreau in a bowl.
2. Peel the oranges and cut into segments, discarding all pith. Cut the melon flesh into cubes or scoop into balls, then add to the bowl with the oranges.
3. Cut the brown ribs from the star fruit, using scissors. Cut the star fruit into slices and add to the bowl.
4. Mix together well, turn into a glass serving dish and sprinkle with the lemon balm. Chill until required.

HOT DESSERTS

STUFFED PEACHES

A well-known Italian recipe which is delicious served warm, or cold with Melba Sauce*.

*4 large firm peaches,
halved and stoned
50 g (2 oz) macaroons,
crushed*

*1 egg white
2 teaspoons caster sugar
2 tablespoons chopped
almonds*

Serves 4
Preparation time:
15 minutes
Cooking time:
30 minutes
Freezing:
Not recommended

1. Scoop out a little flesh from the hollows in the peaches and mash with a fork.
2. Place in a bowl with the macaroon crumbs, egg white and sugar and mix together.
3. Divide the mixture between the peaches and shape into mounds. Sprinkle with the almonds.
4. Place in a buttered ovenproof dish and bake in a preheated oven, 180°C/350°F/Gas Mark 4, for 30 minutes. Serve warm or cold.

CHERRY CLAFOUTIS

A traditional French pudding made with fresh black cherries. If unobtainable, use a 425 g (15 oz) can drained black cherries instead.

*625 g (1¼ lb) black
cherries, stoned
50 g (2 oz) plain flour,
sifted*

*50 g (2 oz) caster sugar
3 eggs
300 ml (½ pint) milk
few drops vanilla essence*

Serves 6
Preparation time:
15 minutes
Cooking time:
About 35–40
minutes
Freezing:
Not recommended

1. Place the cherries in a single layer in a 20 cm (8 inch) flan dish.
2. Place the flour and sugar in a mixing bowl and make a well in the centre. Add the eggs and half of the milk and beat together, gradually incorporating all the flour.
3. Add the remaining milk and the vanilla essence, then pour over the cherries. Bake in a preheated oven, 190°C/375°F/Gas Mark 5, for about 35–40 minutes, until puffed up and golden brown.
4. Serve with smatana if you wish.

HOT BLACKCURRANT COMPOTE

This very easy and quickly prepared dessert is particularly luscious with the geranium leaf flavour.

500 g (1 lb) blackcurrants
4 tablespoons clear honey
2 tablespoons freshly
*   squeezed orange juice*

2 lemon-scented geranium
*   leaves (optional)*

Serves 4
Preparation time:
5 minutes
Cooking time:
15 minutes
Freezing:
Recommended

1. Place all the ingredients in a pan and cook very gently for about 15 minutes, until softened.
2. Remove the geranium leaves, if used. Leave to cool slightly, then spoon into individual glass dishes. Serve with smatana or cream.

DRUNKEN PLUMS

500 g (1 lb) plums or
*   damsons*

3 tablespoons clear honey
3 tablespoons port

Serves 4
Preparation time:
10 minutes
Cooking time:
30–40 minutes
Freezing:
Recommended

1. Make a slit in the side of each plum along the natural division of the fruit.
2. Place in an ovenproof dish and drizzle over the honey. Pour over the port, cover and cook in a preheated oven, 170°C/325°F/Gas Mark 3, for 30–40 minutes, depending on the ripeness of the fruit.
3. Serve with whipped cream or soured cream.

FRUITS DE SAISON GRILLÉS

½ small pineapple, peeled
*   and cored*
125 g (4 oz) strawberries,
*   halved*
2 nectarines, halved,
*   stoned and sliced*

2 kiwi fruit, peeled and
*   sliced*
250 ml (8 fl oz) double
*   cream*
2 tablespoons caster sugar

Serves 4
Preparation time:
10 minutes
Cooking time:
2–3 minutes
Freezing:
Not recommended

1. Cut the pineapple into thin slices, then halve the slices.
2. Arrange attractively on individual heatproof plates with the other fruits.
3. Pour over the cream and sprinkle with the sugar.
4. Place under a preheated very hot grill for 2–3 minutes, until beginning to caramelize. Serve immediately.

BROCHETTES DES FRUITS

A very quick dessert, but most attractive to serve. Especially delicious if served flambéd, but also good with Mango Sauce*.

½ pineapple
12 strawberries
½ × 425 g (15 oz) can
  lychees in syrup, drained
125 g (4 oz) black grapes,
  seeded

2 tablespoons caster sugar
3 tablespoons brandy
strawberry leaves to
  decorate

Serves 6
Preparation time:
15 minutes
Cooking time:
1 minute
Freezing:
Not recommended

1. Peel the pineapple, remove and discard the central hard core, then cut the flesh into chunks.
2. Thread all of the fruit, alternately, onto 12 wooden skewers. Place in the grill pan and sprinkle with the sugar.
3. Place under a preheated hot grill for about 1 minute until heated; do not overcook. Arrange on a heatproof dish.
4. Warm the brandy in a ladle or small saucepan, ignite and pour over the fruit. Decorate with strawberry leaves and serve immediately.

HUNZA APRICOT COMPOTE

These tiny little apricots grow wild in the Hunza Valley of Northern India. They are a rather dull brown colour because they have been dried naturally—not treated to preserve their colour, as is the usual practice with dried apricots. They are extremely sweet and therefore need no added sugar.

250 g (8 oz) Hunza
  apricots
150 ml (¼ pint) pure
  orange juice

300 ml (½ pint) water
8 kumquats, sliced thinly
2 tablespoons toasted
  flaked almonds
  (optional)

Serves 4
Preparation time:
10 minutes, plus
soaking time
Cooking time:
15 minutes
Freezing:
Not recommended

1. Soak the apricots in the orange juice and water for 2 hours.
2. Bring to the boil, then simmer gently for 10 minutes. Add the kumquats and simmer for 5 minutes.
3. Turn into a serving bowl and sprinkle with the almonds if using. Serve with smatana, yogurt or whipped cream.

BLACKCURRANT CRUMBLE

500 g (1 lb) blackcurrants
3 tablespoons clear honey
175 g (6 oz) wholemeal
flour
75 g (3 oz) margarine

50 g (2 oz) muscovado
sugar
50 g (2 oz) hazelnuts,
chopped

1. Place the blackcurrants in a 900 ml (1½ pint) ovenproof dish and drizzle over the honey.
2. Place the flour in a bowl and rub in the margarine until the mixture resembles breadcrumbs. Stir in the sugar and hazelnuts, then sprinkle over the fruit.
3. Bake in a preheated oven, 200°C/400°F/Gas Mark 6, for 25–30 minutes, until golden. Serve with smatana, yogurt or single cream.

Serves 4
Preparation time:
15 minutes
Cooking time:
25–30 minutes
Freezing:
Recommended

CRÊPES AUX PETITS SUISSES

FOR THE BATTER:	*12 Petits Suisses or 350 g*
125 g (4 oz) wholemeal	*(12 oz) natural fromage*
flour	*frais*
1 teaspoon ground	*1 tablespoon clear honey*
cinnamon	*TO FINISH:*
300 ml (½ pint) milk	*25 g (1 oz) butter, melted*
1 egg	*icing sugar to sprinkle*
1 tablespoon oil	*3 tablespoons Grand*
FOR THE FILLING:	*Marnier*
1 orange	*orange slices to decorate*

Serves 6
Preparation time:
25 minutes, plus
standing time for
batter
Cooking time:
8–10 minutes
Freezing:
Recommended for
pancakes only

1. Place the batter ingredients in a food processor or blender and work until smooth. Pour into a jug and leave to stand for 30 minutes.
2. Heat a 15 cm (6 inch) omelette pan and add a few drops of oil. Pour in 1 tablespoon of the batter and tilt the pan to coat the bottom evenly. Cook until the underside is brown, then turn over and cook for 10 seconds. Turn onto a plate.
3. Repeat with the remaining batter, turning each crêpe out onto the plate and separating with greaseproof paper, to make 12 crêpes.
4. Grate the rind from the orange, then peel and divide into segments, discarding all pith.
5. Place the Petits Suisses or fromage frais in a bowl, add the honey and orange rind and mix well.
6. Spoon a tablespoon of the mixture onto each crêpe and place 1 or 2 orange segments on top. Fold into quarters to make a triangle, enclosing the filling.
7. Place on a greased baking sheet, brush with the butter and sprinkle with icing sugar. Bake in a preheated oven, 200°C/400°F/Gas Mark 6, for 8–10 minutes.
8. Sprinkle the liqueur over the crêpes. Decorate with orange slices and serve immediately, on warmed plates.

TARTES AUX POMMES CHAUDES

Attractive individual apple tarts to serve with cream or smatana on cooler summer days.

350 g (12 oz) packet frozen	*2 tablespoons caster sugar*
puff pastry, thawed	*pinch of grated nutmeg*
750 g (1½ lb) dessert	*(optional)*
apples, peeled, quartered	*4 tablespoons Calvados or*
and cored	*brandy*

1. Roll out the pastry thinly on a floured surface to a 5 mm (¼ inch) thickness and cut out four 15 cm (6 inch) circles. Place on a baking sheet and chill for 20 minutes.

2. Slice the apples thinly and arrange overlapping in concentric circles over the pastry rounds. Sprinkle with the sugar and a little nutmeg if wished.

3. Bake in a preheated oven, 220°C/425°F/Gas Mark 7, for 15–20 minutes, until the apples are tinged brown. Place on individual plates.

4. Heat the Calvados or brandy in a ladle or small pan, then ignite. Pour the flaming liquid over the tarts and serve immediately.

Serves 4
Preparation time:
30 minutes, plus chilling pastry
Cooking time:
15–20 minutes
Freezing:
Not recommended

CREAMS, MOUSSES & SOUFFLÉS

LEMON SYLLABUB

One of the most refreshing desserts—ideal to serve after a rich main course. It can also be made with oranges for a change.

6 tablespoons white wine
3 tablespoons clear honey
finely grated rind and
juice of 1 lemon

284 ml (10 fl oz) carton
double cream
1 egg white
lemon rind shreds (see
page 8) to decorate

Serves 4
Preparation time:
15 minutes, plus soaking time and chilling
Freezing:
Not recommended

1. Place the wine, 1 tablespoon of the honey, the lemon rind and juice in a bowl and leave to soak for about 1 hour.
2. Whip the cream until stiff, then gradually whisk in the wine mixture.
3. Whisk the egg white until stiff, then whisk in the remaining honey. Carefully fold into the cream mixture and spoon into 4 glass dishes. Chill for 30 minutes, or until required.
4. Decorate with lemon rind to serve.

PEACH AND MACAROON MOUSSE

Homemade macaroons are best for this dessert, but you can use ratafias if you wish. Peaches vary in sweetness, so you might find you need a little more or less honey.

4 peaches
1 tablespoon clear honey
142 ml (5 fl oz) carton
double cream, lightly
whipped

50 g (2 oz) macaroons,
broken into pieces
2 tablespoons toasted
flaked almonds
(optional)

Serves 4
Preparation time:
20 minutes
Freezing:
Not recommended

1. Cut 12 thin slices from 1 peach and set aside for decoration. Peel and chop the remaining peaches.
2. Place half of the chopped peaches and the honey in a blender or food processor and work until smooth.
3. Fold into the cream with the macaroons and remaining chopped peaches.
4. Spoon into 4 glass dishes and sprinkle with the almonds if using. Decorate with the reserved peach slices.

MANGO AND LIME WHIP

I think mangoes are the most delicious of fruits, tasting somewhere between a strong peach and an orange. Their flavour is enhanced by the use of lime.

2 mangoes
3 tablespoons clear honey
juice of 1 lime

284 ml (10 fl oz) carton
double cream, whipped
1 egg white

Serves 6
Preparation time:
20 minutes
Freezing:
Recommended

1. Cut the mangoes either side of the stone; remove 3 slices of mango, cut in half and set aside for decoration. Scoop out all the flesh and place in a blender or food processor. Add the honey and lime juice and work until smooth. Fold into the cream carefully.
2. Whisk the egg white until stiff, then fold into the mango cream.
3. Spoon into glass serving dishes and decorate with the reserved mango slices.

CRUNCHY GOOSEBERRY WHIP

This dessert looks very attractive served in tall glasses.

500 g (1 lb) gooseberries
3 tablespoons clear honey
284 ml (10 fl oz) carton
double cream, whipped
40 g (1½ oz) butter or
margarine

75 g (3 oz) wholemeal
breadcrumbs
25 g (1 oz) hazelnuts,
chopped and toasted
2 tablespoons demerara
sugar

Serves 4
Preparation time:
20 minutes
Cooking time:
15 minutes
Freezing:
Not recommended

1. Place the gooseberries in a pan with 1 tablespoon water, cover and cook gently for 15 minutes, until soft.
2. Cool slightly, then purée in a blender or food processor; sieve to remove the tops and tails. Add the honey and leave to cool, then stir in the whipped cream.
3. Melt the butter or margarine in a frying pan, add the breadcrumbs and fry until golden brown. Leave to cool, then stir in the hazelnuts and sugar.
4. Divide half of the gooseberry whip between 4 glasses and cover with half of the crumbs. Repeat the layers, finishing with crumbs.

JUNKET

Once such a popular dessert, but one we seldom see nowadays. Very simple to make and delicious served with red fruit compotes or simply with cream.

600 ml (1 pint) milk
1 tablespoon caster sugar
1 teaspoon rennet

1 tablespoon rosewater
grated nutmeg to finish

1. Place the milk and sugar in a heavy-based pan and heat gently, stirring until the sugar has dissolved.
2. Cool the milk to lukewarm, then stir in the rennet and rosewater.
3. Pour into a shallow bowl or individual dishes, cover with muslin or foil and leave to stand at room temperature for 15 minutes, or until set.
4. Sprinkle with nutmeg and chill before serving.

Serves 4
Preparation time: 5 minutes, plus setting and chilling time
Freezing: Not recommended

ST CLEMENTS SOUFFLÉ

3 eggs, separated
125 g (4 oz) caster sugar
grated rind and juice of
*   1 orange and 1 lemon*
1 envelope gelatine,
*   soaked in 3 tablespoons*
*   cold water*
284 ml (10 fl oz) carton
*   double cream, whipped*

TO FINISH:
50 g (2 oz) finely chopped
*   almonds, toasted*
6 tablespoons double
*   cream, whipped*
lemon rind shreds (see
*   page 8)*

Serves 6–8
Preparation time:
45 minutes, plus
setting time
Freezing:
Recommended

1. Tie a double band of foil around the outside of a 15 cm (6 inch) soufflé dish, to stand 5 cm (2 inches) above rim.
2. Place the egg yolks, sugar, and orange and lemon rinds in a bowl. Heat the orange and lemon juice in a small pan until warm, then pour over the egg mixture. Whisk, using an electric mixer, until thick and mousse-like.
3. Heat the gelatine gently until dissolved, then add to the mixture with the cream, folding in carefully.
4. Whisk the egg whites until fairly stiff. Fold 1 tablespoon into the mixture to lighten, then fold in the rest.
5. Turn into the prepared soufflé dish and chill for about 2 hours, until set.
6. Remove the foil carefully, using a hot knife if necessary. Press the chopped almonds around the side. Decorate the top with piped cream and lemon rind shreds.

GOOSEBERRY ELDERFLOWER FOOL

Pick the elderflowers when they are newly in flower.

500 g (1 lb) gooseberries
125 g (4 oz) caster sugar
3 heads elderflower
150 g (5 oz) creamed
*   smatana*

142 ml (5 fl oz) carton
*   double cream, whipped*
frosted leaves (see page 42)
*   to decorate*

Serves 6
Preparation time:
15 minutes
Cooking time:
15 minutes
Freezing:
Recommended

1. Place the gooseberries, sugar, and the elderflower heads tied in muslin in a pan, cover and cook gently for about 15 minutes, until soft.
2. Remove the elderflower heads. Leave the fruit to cool slightly, then purée in a blender or food processor.
3. Fold the smatana into the cream, then fold into the gooseberry purée. Divide between 6 dishes, decorate with frosted leaves and serve with crisp biscuits.

RASPBERRY FOOL AND STRAWBERRIES

*500 g (1 lb) strawberries,
    halved*
250 g (8 oz) raspberries
*3 tablespoons icing sugar,
    sifted*

*284 ml (10 fl oz) carton
    double cream, whipped*
*strawberry leaves to
    decorate*

Serves 6
Preparation time:
15 minutes, plus
chilling
Freezing:
Not recommended

1. Place the strawberries in 6 individual dishes.
2. Rub the raspberries through a nylon sieve, then mix in the icing sugar. Whisk into the cream, then spoon over the strawberries. Chill for at least 20 minutes, then serve, decorated with strawberry leaves.

BLACKCURRANT SOUFFLÉ

If you want to emphasize further the blackcurrant flavour, whip the cream with 2 tablespoons crème de cassis.

*350 g (12 oz)
    blackcurrants*
1 tablespoon clear honey
3 eggs, separated
75 g (3 oz) caster sugar
*1 envelope gelatine,
    soaked in 3 tablespoons
    cold water*

*284 ml (10 fl oz) carton
    double cream, whipped*
TO FINISH:
*50 g (2 oz) finely chopped
    almonds, toasted*
*6 tablespoons double
    cream, whipped*
*frosted currant leaves (see
    page 42)*

Serves 8
Preparation time:
45 minutes, plus
setting time
Cooking time:
About 10 minutes
Freezing:
Recommended

1. Tie a double band of foil around the outside of a 15 cm (6 inch) soufflé dish, to stand 5 cm (2 inches) above rim.
2. Place the blackcurrants in a pan with the honey and 2 tablespoons water, cover and simmer for about 10 minutes, until softened. Leave to cool, then purée in a blender or food processor; sieve to remove the pips.
3. Place the egg yolks and caster sugar in a bowl and whisk with an electric beater until thick and mousse-like.
4. Heat the gelatine gently until dissolved, then add to the blackcurrant purée. Fold into the mousse with the cream.
5. Whisk the egg whites until fairly stiff. Fold 1 tablespoon into the mixture to lighten, then fold in the rest.
6. Turn into the prepared soufflé dish and chill for about 2 hours, until set.
7. Remove the foil carefully, using a hot knife if necessary. Press the chopped almonds around the side. Decorate the top with piped cream and frosted currant leaves.

RASPBERRY TANSY

Tansies were popular in the 17th century. They took their name from the pungent herb which originally flavoured them. They were made with custard, but I have substituted fromage frais in order to cut down the fat content —it is also much quicker made this way.

250 g (8 oz) raspberries
250 g (8 oz) natural
  fromage frais

3 tablespoons clear honey
142 ml (5 fl oz) carton
  double cream, whipped

1. Sieve the raspberries; reserve 3 tablespoons of the purée and gradually mix the rest with the fromage frais and honey, until smooth.
2. Fold in the cream, then divide between 6 glass dishes.
3. Lightly fold a dessertspoonful of the reserved purée into each dessert, to give a marbled effect.

Serves 6
Preparation time:
15 minutes
Freezing:
Not recommended

CHEESE & YOGURT DESSERTS

BLACKBERRY BRÛLÉES

Any red fruit can be used instead of blackberries.

227 g (8 oz) carton cream
    cheese
4 tablespoons natural
    yogurt
1 tablespoon rosewater
2 teaspoons clear honey

125 g (4 oz) blackberries
3 tablespoons chopped
    almonds
2 tablespoons light brown
    soft sugar

Serves 4
Preparation time:
15 minutes, plus
chilling
Freezing:
Not recommended

1. Place the cream cheese, yogurt, rosewater and honey in a bowl and mix together until smooth.
2. Divide the blackberries between 4 ramekins and cover with the cheese mixture, smoothing the tops.
3. Mix the almonds with the sugar and sprinkle over the top of each ramekin to cover completely.
4. Place under a preheated hot grill for 2–3 minutes, until the sugar caramelizes. Chill for 30 minutes before serving.

RASPBERRY GLORY

A healthier version of knickerbocker glory! Make it with
any soft fruit of your choice.

250 g (8 oz) raspberries
227 g (8 oz) carton curd
    cheese
1 tablespoon clear honey

300 g (10 oz) creamed
    smatana or Greek
    yogurt
2 tablespoons chopped
    almonds, toasted

Serves 4
Preparation time:
15 minutes
Freezing:
Not recommended

1. Rub half of the raspberries through a sieve to make a purée. Gradually add the curd cheese and honey and mix until smooth.
2. Divide a third of the whole raspberries between tall glasses, then add a spoonful of the raspberry cheese to each.
3. Stir the smatana or yogurt until smooth, then spoon half over the cheese mixture. Repeat the layers. Arrange the remaining raspberries on top and spoon over the rest of the raspberry cheese.
4. Decorate with the chopped almonds to serve.

RASPBERRY CHEESECAKE

25 g (1 oz) butter, melted
125 g (4 oz) digestive
    biscuits, crushed
350 g (12 oz) raspberries
350 g (12 oz) natural
    fromage frais

2 tablespoons clear honey
1 tablespoon gelatine,
    soaked in 3 tablespoons
    water
142 ml (5 fl oz) carton
    double cream, whipped

Serves 8
Preparation time:
30 minutes, plus
setting time
Freezing:
Recommended

1. Combine the butter and biscuit crumbs. Press over the base of a 20 cm (8 inch) loose-bottomed cake tin. Chill until firm.
2. Meanwhile, rub the raspberries through a nylon sieve.
3. Place the fromage frais and honey in a bowl, blend well, then stir in all but 2 tablespoons of the raspberry purée.
4. Heat the gelatine gently until dissolved, then stir into the raspberry mixture.
5. Fold in the cream, then spoon over the crumb base, smoothing the surface. Spoon the remaining purée into a greaseproof paper piping bag and pipe a series of circles on top. Use a skewer to swirl the purée into a pattern.
6. Chill in the refrigerator for about 1 hour, until set. Remove from the tin and place on a plate to serve.

STRAWBERRY CHEESE PUFFS

250 g (8.8 oz) packet
    puff pastry
beaten egg to glaze
2 tablespoons chopped
    almonds

FOR THE FILLING:
175 g (6 oz) natural
    fromage frais
1 teaspoon clear honey
125 g (4 oz) strawberries,
    sliced

Makes 5 puffs
Preparation time:
15 minutes, plus
chilling
Cooking time:
8–10 minutes
Freezing:
Not recommended

1. Roll the pastry out very thinly on a floured surface into a rectangle measuring 25 × 38 cm (10 × 15 inches). Cut in half lengthways, then cut into ten 7.5 cm (3 inch) wide rectangles. Place well apart on baking sheets and chill for 15 minutes.
2. Brush half of the pastry rectangles with beaten egg and sprinkle with the almonds. Bake all of the rectangles in a preheated oven, 220°C/425°F/Gas Mark 7, for 8–10 minutes, until golden brown and crisp right through. Cool on a wire rack.
3. Mix the fromage frais and honey together and place a spoonful on each plain pastry rectangle. Arrange some strawberries on top, then cover with the nutty rectangles.

APPLE AND BLACKBERRY CHEESE

I like to use Cox's Orange Pippins or Russets for their flavour in this recipe.

350 g (12 oz) dessert apples, peeled, cored and sliced
175 g (6 oz) blackberries
1 tablespoon clear honey

227 g (8 oz) carton cream cheese
frosted leaves (see page 42) to decorate

1. Place the apples, blackberries and honey in a heavy-based pan, cover and simmer for 15 minutes, until soft.
2. Cool slightly, then place in a blender or food processor and work until smooth. Sieve to remove the seeds.
3. Place the cream cheese in a bowl and gradually mix in the fruit purée, until blended.
4. Spoon into 4 dishes and decorate with frosted leaves.

Serves 4
Preparation time: 15 minutes
Cooking time: 15 minutes
Freezing: Recommended

CRÈME SUCRÉE

A light, refreshing dessert which can be assembled in minutes. Crème Sucrée is equally delicious served with strawberries or other soft fruit.

284 ml (10 fl oz) carton double cream
2 × 150 g (5.3 oz) cartons natural set yogurt

2 tablespoons muscovado sugar

Serves 4
Preparation time:
10 minutes, plus chilling
Freezing:
Not recommended

1. Whip the cream until it stands in stiff peaks. Fold in the yogurt, then spoon into 4 glass dishes.
2. Sprinkle with the sugar and chill for 1 hour to dissolve the sugar, before serving.

CŒURS À LA CRÈME

These heart-shaped desserts come from France, where they are served with pouring cream. They are also delicious served with strawberries, but I like them best with Strawberry or Melba Sauce. If you do not have the little heart-shaped moulds, you can drain the cheese mixture in a muslin-lined nylon sieve, turn it out whole, and serve it cut into wedges.

300 g (10 oz) natural fromage frais
2 teaspoons clear honey
142 ml (5 fl oz) carton double cream, whipped

150 ml (¼ pint) Strawberry or Melba Sauce* to serve

Serves 4
Preparation time:
25 minutes, plus overnight draining
Freezing:
Not recommended

1. Mix the fromage frais and honey together until smooth, then fold in the cream.
2. Line 4 heart-shaped moulds with muslin, spoon in the cheese mixture and smooth the tops. Place on a plate in the refrigerator and leave to drain overnight.
3. Turn the desserts onto individual plates and pour a little strawberry or Melba sauce around each one.

COINTREAU CURD CUPS

1 orange
227 g (8 oz) carton curd
   cheese
2 tablespoons clear honey

1 tablespoon Cointreau
125 g (4 oz) smatana
1 egg white

Serves 4
Preparation time:
10 minutes, plus
chilling
Freezing:
Not recommended

1. Grate the rind coarsely from a quarter of the orange and set aside for decoration. Grate the remaining rind finely.
2. Place the curd cheese in a bowl, then beat in the grated orange rind, honey and Cointreau.
3. Gradually mix in the smatana until smooth.
4. Whisk the egg white until it forms stiff peaks, then carefully fold into the cheese mixture.
5. Spoon into 4 custard cups, glass dishes or ramekins and chill for 15 minutes. Top with the orange shreds to serve.

LEMON CHEESECAKE

50 g (2 oz) butter
175 g (6 oz) digestive
   biscuits, crushed
2 × 227 g (8 oz) cartons
   curd cheese
2 tablespoons clear honey
300 g (10 oz) creamed
   smatana

3 eggs, separated
grated rind and juice of
   1 large lemon
1 tablespoon gelatine,
   soaked in 3 tablespoons
   water
lemon rind shreds (see
   page 8) to decorate

Serves 8
Preparation time:
35 minutes, plus
setting time
Freezing:
Recommended

1. Melt the butter in a pan, then stir in the biscuit crumbs. Press over the base of a 20 cm (8 inch) loose-bottomed cake tin. Chill until firm.
2. Meanwhile, place the curd cheese, honey and smatana in a bowl and mix together until smooth. Set aside a quarter of this mixture for decoration.
3. Add the egg yolks and grated lemon rind and juice to the remaining mixture and mix well.
4. Heat the gelatine gently until dissolved, then add to the lemon mixture.
5. Whisk the egg whites until stiff, then fold into the mixture. Pour over the crumb base.
6. Chill for about 2 hours, until set.
7. Remove from the tin and place the cheesecake on a serving plate. Place the reserved cheese mixture in a piping bag fitted with a fluted nozzle and pipe a border around the edge. Decorate with lemon shreds.

YOGURT FRUIT SALAD

A quick and easy dessert; use any combination of fruit.

*2 × 150 g (5.3 oz) cartons
    natural yogurt*
2 teaspoons clear honey
1 banana

*250 g (8 oz) strawberries,
    sliced*
*2 tablespoons flaked
    almonds, toasted*

1. Mix the yogurt and honey together until smooth.
2. Slice the banana and fold into the yogurt mixture with the strawberries.
3. Spoon into 4 wine glasses or individual dishes and sprinkle with the almonds to serve.

Serves 4
Preparation time:
10 minutes
Freezing:
Not recommended

SORBETS

MELON WITH RASPBERRY SORBET

If you have time, scoop out the melon flesh with a melon baller and chill in the refrigerator. Serve the scoops of sorbet and melon in the melon shell.

2 small, very ripe
Charentais melons,
chilled
1/2 quantity Raspberry
Sorbet (page 48)

2 tablespoons framboise
liqueur or kirsch
frosted raspberry leaves
(see below)

Serves 4
Preparation time:
10 minutes, plus
making sorbet
Freezing:
Not recommended

1. Cut the melons in half, scoop out and discard the seeds. Cut a thin slice from the base of each half so that they stand firmly.
2. Scoop some raspberry sorbet into each cavity, pour over a little liqueur and decorate with frosted leaves. Serve immediately.

To prepare frosted leaves and fruit: Brush the chosen leaves or fruit with egg white, then dip in caster sugar to coat. Place on greaseproof paper and leave for 1–2 hours, until dry. Use to decorate desserts.

KIWI SHERBET

Make sure the fruit is soft so that the fragrance, which only comes with ripeness, has developed.

3 kiwi fruit, peeled
350 ml (12 fl oz) pure
apple juice

2 tablespoons clear honey
1 egg white

Serves 6
Preparation time:
10 minutes
Freezing time:
About 5 hours

1. Mash the kiwi fruit with a fork to form a purée. Mix with the apple juice and honey, then pour into a rigid freezer-proof container. Cover, seal and freeze for about 3 hours, until slushy. Turn into a bowl.
2. Whisk the egg whites until fairly stiff, then whisk into the kiwi ice. Return to the container, cover, seal and freeze for about 2 hours, until firm.
3. Transfer to the refrigerator 20 minutes before serving, to soften. Scoop into chilled glasses to serve.

ROSE HIP SORBET

Any of the perfumed teas may be used for making sorbets
—they have beautifully delicate flavours.

3 sachets rose hip tea
450 ml (3/4 pint) boiling
  water
75 g (3 oz) caster sugar

juice of 1/2 lemon
1 tablespoon rosewater
1 egg white

Serves 4
Preparation time:
20 minutes
Freezing time:
About 5 hours

1. Place the tea sachets in a jug and pour on the boiling
water. Add the sugar and set aside for 10 minutes.
2. Remove the tea sachets, then add the lemon juice and
rosewater and pour into a rigid, freezerproof container.
Cover, seal and freeze for about 3 hours, until half-frozen.
Turn into a bowl.
3. Whisk the egg white until stiff, then whisk into the
half-frozen sorbet. Return to the container, cover, seal and
freeze for about 2 hours, until firm.
4. Transfer to the refrigerator 10 minutes before serving,
to soften. Scoop into chilled glasses to serve.

GUAVA SORBET

Canned guavas make a very good sorbet. Their subtle
perfumed flavour is enhanced by the passion fruit.

411 g (14 1/2 oz) can
  guavas in syrup
150 ml (1/4 pint) pure
  orange juice

50 g (2 oz) icing sugar
2 passion fruit
1 egg white

Serves 4
Preparation time:
20 minutes
Freezing time:
About 5 hours

1. Place the guavas and their syrup, orange juice and icing
sugar in a blender or food processor and work until
smooth; sieve to remove the seeds.
2. Halve the passion fruit and scoop the flesh into a sieve
over a bowl. Press through the sieve to extract as much
juice as possible. Stir into the guava purée.
3. Pour into a rigid freezerproof container, cover, seal and
freeze for about 3 hours, until slushy. Turn into a bowl.
4. Whisk the egg white until stiff, then whisk into the
half-frozen guava purée. Return to the container, cover,
seal and freeze for about 2 hours, until firm.
5. Transfer to the refrigerator 20 minutes before serving,
to soften. Scoop into chilled glasses or shape into ovals
using 2 dessertspoons, then arrange on 4 chilled plates.

WILLIAM PEAR SORBET

750 g (1½ lb) ripe William pears, peeled, quartered and cored	Eau de Vie de Poires Williams liqueur (optional)
150 ml (¼ pint) pure apple juice	1 egg white
75 g (3 oz) caster sugar	TO SERVE:
	1 William pear, cored, sliced and sprinkled with lemon juice

Serves 4
Preparation time:
20 minutes
Cooking time:
10–15 minutes
Freezing time:
About 5 hours

1. Place the pears, apple juice and sugar in a pan, cover and simmer gently for 10–15 minutes, until soft. Pour into a food processor or blender and work until smooth.
2. Pour into a rigid freezerproof container and leave to cool. Add the liqueur, if using, then cover, seal and freeze for about 3 hours, until half-frozen. Turn into a bowl.
3. Whisk the egg white until stiff, then whisk into the half-frozen pear purée. Return to the container, cover, seal and freeze for about 2 hours, until firm.
4. Transfer to the refrigerator 20 minutes before serving, to soften.
5. Shape the sorbet into ovals, using 2 dessertspoons, and arrange on 4 chilled plates with the pear slices to serve.

GERANIUM LEAF WATER ICE

The leaves of the sweet-scented geranium give a lovely perfume and flavour to this sorbet. There are many varieties, all with different perfumes.

450 ml (³⁄₄ pint) water
125 g (4 oz) caster sugar
thinly pared rind and juice
* of 2 lemons*

3 sweet-scented geranium
* leaves*
1 egg white
tiny geranium leaves to
* decorate*

1. Place the water, sugar, lemon rind and geranium leaves in a pan and heat gently, stirring until the sugar has dissolved. Bring to the boil, then simmer for 5 minutes. Add the lemon juice, cover and leave to cool.
2. Strain into a rigid freezerproof container, cover, seal and freeze for about 3 hours, until half-frozen. Turn into a bowl.
3. Whisk the egg white until stiff, then whisk into the half-frozen ice. Return to the container, cover, seal and freeze for about 2 hours, until firm.
4. Transfer to the refrigerator 20 minutes before serving, to soften. Scoop into chilled glasses and decorate with geranium leaves to serve.

Serves 6
Preparation time:
20 minutes
Freezing time:
About 5 hours

RASPBERRY SORBET

The flavour of this sorbet is improved if you add 2 tablespoons framboise liqueur with the honey.

500 g (1 lb) raspberries
300 ml (½ pint) water
6 tablespoons clear honey

1 egg white
raspberry or mint leaves to decorate

Serves 6
Preparation time:
15 minutes
Freezing time:
About 5 hours

1. Purée the raspberries in a blender or food processor. Rub through a nylon sieve to remove the pips.
2. Mix the purée with the water and honey and pour into a rigid freezerproof container. Cover, seal and freeze for about 3 hours, until half-frozen. Turn into a bowl.
3. Whisk the egg white until stiff, then whisk into the half-frozen raspberry purée. Return to the container, cover, seal and freeze for about 2 hours, until firm.
4. Ten minutes before serving, scoop onto chilled plates, with a melon baller if you have one, and place in the refrigerator to soften. Decorate with raspberry or mint leaves.

ORANGE GRANITA

A very refreshing water ice that originates in Italy. Granitas are less sweet and more crumbly in texture than sorbets; they are ideal to serve after a very rich meal.

125 g (4 oz) caster sugar
600 ml (1 pint) water
thinly pared rind and juice
of 2 oranges

thinly pared rind and juice
of 1 lemon
2 tablespoons Cointreau
frosted leaves (see page 42)
to decorate

Serves 4
Preparation time:
20 minutes
Freezing time:
About 6 hours

1. Place the sugar, water, and orange and lemon rinds in a saucepan and heat gently, stirring until the sugar has dissolved, then boil for 5 minutes. Add the fruit juices and leave to cool.
2. Strain into a rigid freezerproof container, cover, seal and freeze for about 3 hours, until half-frozen. Remove from the freezer, whisk well, then return to the freezer for a further 3 hours.
3. Leave at room temperature for 15 minutes, then stir until crumbly. Spoon into tall glasses, pour over a little Cointreau and decorate with the frosted leaves.

BOÎTE AUX FRAISES

Always an impressive dessert to serve when strawberries are in season. The chocolate squares can be made in advance and stored in an airtight container.

3 eggs
125 g (4 oz) light brown
  soft sugar
75 g (3 oz) wholemeal
  flour
TO FINISH:
125 g (4 oz) plain
  chocolate, melted
3 tablespoons framboise
  liqueur or Grand
  Marnier

250 g (8 oz) strawberries
2 tablespoons icing sugar
142 ml (5 fl oz) carton
  double cream
150 g (5.3 oz) carton
  natural set yogurt
frosted leaves (see page 42)
  to decorate

Serves 6
Preparation time:
45 minutes
Cooking time:
30–35 minutes
Freezing:
Not recommended

1. Grease and line a 20 cm (8 inch) square cake tin.
2. Whisk the eggs and sugar together using an electric whisk for about 10 minutes, until the mixture is very thick and mousse-like.
3. Carefully fold in the flour, then turn into the prepared tin. Bake in a preheated oven, 190°C/375°F/Gas Mark 5, for 30–35 minutes, until the cake springs back when lightly pressed. Cool on a wire rack.
4. Pour the melted chocolate onto greaseproof paper and leave until just set. Cut into 5 cm (2 inch) squares, using a sharp knife and ruler.
5. Sprinkle the liqueur over the sponge and place on a serving plate. Set aside 4 strawberries for decoration. Slice the remainder, sprinkle with half of the icing sugar and mix together gently. Spoon on top of the sponge.
6. Whip the cream with the remaining sugar until stiff. Mix the yogurt with a fork until smooth, then carefully fold into the cream.
7. Spread some of the cream mixture over the sides of the cake. Cover with the chocolate squares, overlapping slightly.
8. Place the remaining cream mixture in a piping bag fitted with a fluted nozzle and pipe over the fruit. Cut the reserved strawberries in half and arrange on top of the gâteau. Decorate with frosted leaves.

STRAWBERRY ROULADE

The light sponge roll is made with ground almonds. Any soft fruit can be used for the filling.

3 eggs
125 g (4 oz) caster sugar
50 g (2 oz) plain flour,
sifted
50 g (2 oz) ground
almonds

1 tablespoon hot water
icing sugar for dredging
FOR THE FILLING:
250 g (8 oz) strawberries
284 ml (10 fl oz) double
cream, lightly whipped

Serves 8
Preparation time:
45 minutes
Cooking time:
8–10 minutes
Freezing:
Not recommended

1. Grease and line a 30 × 20 cm (12 × 8 inch) Swiss roll tin.
2. Whisk eggs and sugar together using an electric whisk, until very thick and mousse-like. Carefully fold in the flour and almonds, adding the water when almost folded in.
3. Turn the mixture into the prepared tin and bake in a preheated oven, 200°C/400°F/Gas Mark 6, for 8–10 minutes, until the cake springs back when lightly pressed.
4. Wring out a clean tea-towel in hot water and lay it on a work surface. Place a sheet of greaseproof paper on top and sprinkle it with icing sugar.
5. Turn the sponge out onto the paper and remove the lining paper. Trim off the crisp sides of the cake, then roll up with the paper inside the sponge. Place on a wire rack with the join underneath and leave to cool.
6. Set aside a few strawberries and a quarter of the cream for decoration. Chop the remaining strawberries and fold into the rest of the cream.
7. Unroll the sponge and remove the greaseproof paper. Spread the strawberry cream mixture evenly over the sponge and roll up again. Place on a serving dish and pipe the reserved cream along the top. Halve the reserved strawberries and use to decorate the roulade.

ICED MERINGUE GÂTEAU

4 egg whites
250 g (8 oz) caster sugar
125 g (4 oz) ground
almonds
FOR THE FILLING:
1 small pineapple, halved,
cored and cut up
2 tablespoons kirsch
1 egg white

2 tablespoons clear honey
250 ml (8 fl oz) double
cream, whipped
TO FINISH:
142 ml (5 fl oz) carton
double cream, whipped
50 g (2 oz) flaked
almonds, toasted
icing sugar to sprinkle

1. Whisk the egg whites until stiff and dry, then whisk in 4 tablespoons of the sugar. Carefully fold in the remaining sugar and the ground almonds.

2. Put the meringue into a piping bag fitted with a 1 cm (½ inch) plain nozzle and pipe into three 20 cm (8 inch) rounds on baking sheets lined with silicone paper.

3. Bake in a very cool oven, 130°C/250°F/Gas Mark ½, for 2 hours. Cool on the baking sheets, then peel off the paper.

4. To make the filling, put the pineapple in a food processor or blender with the kirsch and work until smooth.

5. Whisk the egg white until stiff, then whisk in the honey. Fold in the pineapple purée and cream.

6. Trim the meringue rounds to fit inside a 20 cm (8 inch) loose-bottomed cake tin and place one meringue round on the base. Spoon over half the pineapple mixture and cover with a second meringue round. Cover with the remaining pineapple mixture and top with the third meringue round. Wrap in a polythene bag, seal and freeze until firm.

7. Remove from the polythene bag and leave to stand at room temperature for 15 minutes. Top with whipped cream and sprinkle with the almonds and icing sugar to serve. Use a hot knife to cut the gâteau cleanly.

Serves 8
Preparation time:
45 minutes
Cooking time:
2 hours
Freezing:
Recommended

STRAWBERRY WALNUT GÂTEAU

3 eggs
125 g (4 oz) light brown
soft sugar
75 g (3 oz) wholemeal
flour
50 g (2 oz) walnuts,
ground

FOR THE FILLING:
284 ml (10 fl oz) carton
double cream, whipped
500 g (1 lb) strawberries,
sliced
50 g (2 oz) chopped
walnuts

Serves 8
Preparation time:
40 minutes
Cooking time:
20–25 minutes
Freezing:
Not recommended

1. Grease and line a 30 × 20 cm (12 × 8 inch) Swiss roll tin.
2. Place the eggs and sugar in a bowl and whisk with an electric whisk for about 10 minutes, until the mixture is very thick and mousse-like.
3. Carefully fold in the flour and ground walnuts.
4. Turn into the prepared tin and bake in a preheated oven, 190°C/375°F/Gas Mark 5, for 20–25 minutes. Turn onto a wire rack to cool.
5. Set aside a quarter of the cream and a few strawberry slices. Fold the other strawberries and cream together.
6. Cut the cake into 3 equal pieces widthways and sandwich together with the strawberry and cream filling.
7. Spread some of the remaining cream over the sides of the gâteau and coat with the chopped walnuts.
8. Spread the rest of the cream over the top of the gâteau and decorate with the remaining strawberry slices.

JOHANNISBER KUCHEN

A delicious redcurrant cake which a German friend of mine serves. You can also use apples, plums or pears.

125 g (4 oz) butter or margarine
125 g (4 oz) caster sugar
finely grated rind and juice of 1 lemon
2 eggs
175 g (6 oz) self-raising flour, sifted

1 tablespoon boiling water
250 g (8 oz) redcurrants
1 tablespoon icing sugar
150 ml (¼ pint) Redcurrant Sauce* to serve

1. Grease and line a 20 cm (8 inch) loose-bottomed cake tin.
2. Cream the fat, sugar and lemon rind together until light and fluffy.
3. Beat in the eggs one at a time, adding a tablespoon of flour with the second egg. Fold in the remaining flour with the lemon juice and finally the water.
4. Turn the mixture into the prepared tin. Arrange the redcurrants over the top and sprinkle with the icing sugar.
5. Bake in a preheated oven, 180°C/350°F/Gas Mark 4, for 50–60 minutes.
6. Leave in the tin for a few minutes, then transfer to a wire rack to cool. Serve sliced, with the redcurrant sauce.

Serves 6–8
Preparation time: 25 minutes
Cooking time: 50–60 minutes
Freezing: Not recommended

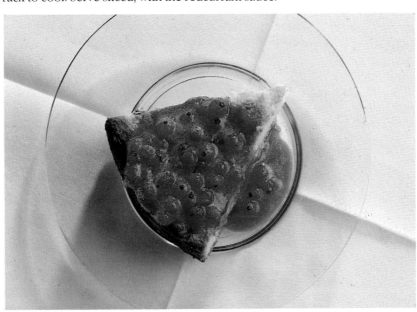

REDCURRANT MERINGUES

The meringue rounds for these attractive individual desserts can be stored in an airtight tin for up to a week.

2 egg whites
125 g (4 oz) caster sugar
FOR THE FILLING:
125 g (4 oz) redcurrants
250 ml (8 fl oz) double
*   cream*

2 tablespoons framboise
*   liqueur (optional)*
2 teaspoons clear honey
125 g (4 oz) raspberries

Serves 8
Preparation time:
35 minutes
Cooking time:
2 hours
Freezing:
Not recommended

1. Whisk the egg whites until stiff, then gradually whisk in the sugar until the mixture holds its shape.
2. Line 2 baking sheets with silicone paper; draw on eight 7.5 cm (3 inch) circles and eight 5 cm (2 inch) circles.
3. Put the meringue mixture into a piping bag fitted with a 1 cm (½ inch) plain nozzle and pipe onto the paper to cover the circles completely.
4. Bake in a preheated oven, 130°C/250°F/Gas Mark ½, for 2 hours. Transfer to a wire rack to cool.
5. Reserve 8 redcurrants for decoration; strip the rest from their stalks.
6. Whip the cream, liqueur if using, and honey together until thickened, then spoon a quarter of it into a piping bag fitted with a large fluted nozzle.
7. Mix the redcurrants and raspberries into the remaining cream and place a spoonful on each of the large meringue circles. Cover with the small circles.
8. Decorate the top circles with the remaining whipped cream and redcurrants. Serve immediately.

GOOSEBERRY CHARLOTTE

Elderflowers impart a delicate flavour to this delicious charlotte. They are best picked when they begin to flower, early in June, and have a creamy appearance.

500 g (1 lb) gooseberries
2 heads elderflower
*   (optional)*
2 eggs, plus 1 yolk
75 g (3 oz) caster sugar
1 envelope gelatine,
*   soaked in 3 tablespoons*
*   cold water*

250 ml (8 fl oz) carton
*   double cream, whipped*
TO FINISH:
30 langue de chat biscuits
1 kiwi fruit, peeled and
*   sliced thinly*

1. Place the gooseberries in a pan with the elderflower heads tied in muslin if using, and 2 tablespoons water. Cover and cook gently for 10–15 minutes, until soft. Remove the elderflowers and cool slightly.

2. Place in a food processor or blender and work until smooth, then sieve to remove the tops and tails.

3. Place the eggs, egg yolk and sugar in a bowl and whisk with an electric mixer until thick and mousse-like.

4. Heat the gelatine gently until dissolved, then mix into the gooseberry purée.

5. Set aside 2 tablespoons of the cream. Fold the gooseberry mixture into the rest, then fold into the egg mixture.

6. Turn into a greased 18 cm (7 inch) loose-bottomed cake tin and chill for 2 hours, until set.

7. Turn out onto a serving dish, spread the reserved cream round the side and press on the biscuits, overlapping them slightly.

8. Decorate the charlotte with the kiwi fruit.

Serves 8
Preparation time:
45 minutes
Setting time:
2 hours
Freezing:
Recommended

FRANGIPANE FLAN

Morello cherries are best for this flan as their sharpness gives the necessary flavour.

RICH SHORTCRUST
PASTRY:
250 g (8 oz) plain flour
150 g (5 oz) butter or
margarine
1 tablespoon caster sugar
1 egg yolk
1–2 tablespoons iced water
beaten egg to glaze

FOR THE FILLING:
1 egg
50 g (2 oz) caster sugar
50 g (2 oz) soft margarine
125 g (4 oz) ground
almonds
2 drops almond essence
340 g (12 oz) can Morello
cherries in syrup,
drained

Serves 8
Preparation time:
40 minutes, plus
chilling pastry
Cooking time:
30–35 minutes
Freezing:
Recommended

1. Sift the flour into a bowl and rub in the butter or margarine until the mixture resembles breadcrumbs. Stir in the sugar. Add the egg yolk and enough water to mix to a firm dough. Turn onto a floured surface and knead lightly until smooth.
2. Cut off two thirds of the dough, roll out thinly on a floured surface and use to line a 20 cm (8 inch) flan ring, placed on a baking sheet. Chill for 30 minutes.
3. Meanwhile, make the filling. Place the egg, sugar, margarine, ground almonds and almond essence in a bowl and beat until smooth.
4. Place the cherries in the flan case and spoon the almond mixture over the top, levelling the surface with a palette knife.
5. Roll the remaining pastry out thinly and cut into narrow strips. Use these to make a lattice pattern over the filling, moistening the edges of the pastry with water. Brush with beaten egg.
6. Bake in a preheated oven, 200°C/400°F/Gas Mark 6, for 20 minutes, then lower the temperature to 190°C/375°F/Gas Mark 5 and bake for 10–15 minutes, until firm to the touch and golden. Serve warm or cold.

GOOSEBERRY CREAM TART

A delicious, creamy tart which can also be made with
apples or apricots.

PÂTE SUCRÉE:
175 g (6 oz) plain flour
75 g (3 oz) butter, softened
75 g (3 oz) caster sugar
3 egg yolks

FOR THE FILLING:
500 g (1 lb) gooseberries
2 tablespoons caster sugar
250 ml (8 fl oz) single
  cream
2 eggs

Serves 8
Preparation time:
30 minutes, plus
chilling pastry
Cooking time:
45 minutes
Freezing:
Recommended

1. Sift the flour onto a cool work surface, make a well in
the centre and put in the butter, sugar and egg yolks.
2. Using the fingertips of one hand, work these ingredients together, then draw in the flour and work to a paste.
Knead lightly until smooth, wrap in a polythene bag and
chill for about 1 hour.
3. Meanwhile prepare the filling. Place the gooseberries,
sugar and 2 tablespoons water in a heavy-based pan, cover
and cook gently for 10 minutes.
4. Mix together the cream and eggs, then add the
gooseberries and mix gently.
5. Turn the dough onto a floured surface, roll out and use
to line a 23 cm (9 inch) fluted flan ring, placed on a baking
sheet. Chill for 15 minutes.
6. Pour the filling into the flan case and bake in a preheated oven, 190°C/375°F/Gas Mark 5, for 45 minutes, until
golden.
7. Remove the flan carefully from the ring. Serve warm or
cold.

BLACKCURRANT FILO FLOWERS

Filo pastry is now becoming increasingly available in
supermarkets. You can make the filo flowers in advance
and store them in an airtight tin, leaving only the filling to
prepare on the day.

250 g (8 oz) filo pastry
250 g (8 oz) blackcurrants
2 dessert apples, peeled
  and chopped
3 tablespoons clear honey
250 ml (8 fl oz) double
  cream, whipped

2 tablespoons pure apple
  juice
2 tablespoons crème de
  cassis (optional)
blackcurrant or mint
  leaves to decorate

1. Cut the filo pastry into twenty-four 10 cm (4 inch) squares. Grease the outside of 8 inverted dariole moulds.
2. Drape 3 squares of filo pastry over each mould, so that the corners are separate and resemble flower petals.
3. Place on a baking sheet and bake in a preheated oven, 190°C/375°F/Gas Mark 5, for 6–8 minutes, until golden brown; make sure they do not overcook.
4. Leave to cool, then lift off the mould and turn up the right way.
5. Place the blackcurrants, apples and honey in a pan, cover and bring to the boil, then simmer gently for 10–15 minutes, until softened.
6. Cool slightly, then purée in a food processor or blender. Rub through a nylon sieve and leave until cold.
7. Fold half of the purée into the cream and divide the mixture between the filo flowers.
8. Stir the apple juice and cassis, if using, into the remaining purée and spoon some onto each serving plate to cover the base. Place a filo flower in the centre of each plate and decorate each with a leaf.

Serves 8
Preparation time:
40 minutes
Cooking time:
8–10 minutes
Freezing:
Not recommended

STRAWBERRY CREAM TARTLETS

PÂTE SUCRÉE:
125 g (4 oz) plain flour
50 g (2 oz) butter, softened
50 g (2 oz) caster sugar
2 egg yolks
FOR THE FILLING:
2 tablespoons single cream

6 Petits Suisses
1 teaspoon clear honey
125 g (4 oz) small
* strawberries, halved*
FOR THE GLAZE:
4 tablespoons redcurrant
* jelly*

Makes 14
Preparation time:
30 minutes, plus
chilling pastry
Cooking time:
10 minutes
Freezing:
Not recommended

1. Make and chill the pâte sucrée as described on page 60. Roll out thinly on a floured surface and use to line 14 patty tins. Press a square of foil into each and chill for 15 minutes.
2. Bake 'blind' in a preheated oven, 190°C/375°F/Gas Mark 5, for 10 minutes or until golden brown. Leave to cool, remove the foil and place on a plate.
3. Mix the cream, Petits Suisses and honey together and spoon a little into each tartlet. Top with the strawberries.
4. Heat the redcurrant jelly until liquid and smooth, then brush generously over the strawberries.

BRAMBLE SCRUNCH

This can be made with any soft red fruit. It can be prepared in individual ramekins if you prefer.

6 tablespoons oil
3 tablespoons clear honey
175 g (6 oz) rolled oats
25 g (1 oz) desiccated
* coconut*

FOR THE TOPPING:
350 g (12 oz) blackberries
150 g (5.3 oz) carton
* natural yogurt*
250 ml (8 fl oz) double
* cream, whipped*

Serves 6
Preparation time:
25 minutes
Cooking time:
30–35 minutes
Freezing:
Not recommended

1. Place the oil and honey in a pan and heat gently. Stir in the oats and coconut and mix thoroughly.
2. Sprinkle into a greased 23 cm (9 inch) round flan dish and fork to the edges.
3. Bake in a preheated oven, 180°C/350°F/Gas Mark 4, for 30–35 minutes, until golden. Leave to cool.
4. Sprinkle all but 8 blackberries over the oat mixture. Rub the 8 blackberries through a sieve and set aside.
5. Mix the yogurt until smooth, then fold into the cream. Spoon over the blackberries and smooth to the edges.
6. Drizzle the reserved blackberry purée over the cream and swirl into a pattern with a skewer. Chill until required.

NECTARINE GALETTES

I like to leave the smooth, colourful skin on the nectarines, but they can, of course, be peeled.

75 g (3 oz) margarine
50 g (2 oz) light brown soft
    sugar
125 g (4 oz) wholemeal
    flour
75 g (3 oz) hazelnuts,
    ground and toasted

FOR THE FILLING:
284 ml (10 fl oz) carton
    double cream
2 tablespoons Grand
    Marnier
5 nectarines
1 tablespoon lemon juice

Makes 10
Preparation time:
35 minutes
Cooking time:
12–15 minutes
Freezing:
Recommended for
pastry only

1. Cream the margarine and sugar together until light and fluffy. Stir in the flour and hazelnuts and mix to a firm dough, using your hand.
2. Turn onto a floured surface and knead lightly until smooth. Roll out the dough thinly and cut out ten 7.5 cm (3 inch) circles and ten 5 cm (2 inch) circles.
3. Place on a baking sheet and bake in a preheated oven, 180°C/350°F/Gas Mark 4, for 12–15 minutes, until golden. Transfer to a wire rack to cool.
4. Whip the cream and liqueur together until soft peaks form. Place in a piping bag fitted with a large fluted nozzle.
5. Cut the nectarines into slices and brush with the lemon juice. Arrange half of the nectarine slices on the larger pastry rounds and cover with piped cream whirls. Arrange the remaining nectarine slices on top and cover with the smaller rounds.
6. Decorate with piped cream rosettes.

PASSION FRUIT BASKETS

These pretty little baskets make ideal containers for mousses, whips and ice creams. The mixture makes fourteen so you will be able to freeze some for future use. Do not fill them more than 30 minutes before serving, or they will lose their crispness.

40 g (1½ oz) plain flour,
    sifted
75 g (3 oz) caster sugar
3 egg whites
25 g (1 oz) butter or
    margarine, melted

FOR THE FILLING:
2 passion fruit
50 g (2 oz) natural
    fromage frais
6 tablespoons double
    cream
2 teaspoons clear honey

1. Mix the flour and sugar together in a bowl, add the egg whites and melted fat, and beat together thoroughly until smooth.

2. Place dessertspoonfuls of the mixture well apart on greased and floured baking sheets; spread them thinly to form 13 cm (5 inch) rounds. Bake one batch at a time in a preheated oven, 200°C/400°F/Gas Mark 6, for 4–5 minutes, until golden at the edges.

3. Leave the biscuits to cool slightly, then carefully remove each one from the baking sheets with a sharp knife. Place each biscuit top side down over the base of an inverted glass. Mould the biscuit to give wavy edges, leave to set, then remove carefully.

4. To make the filling, cut the passion fruit in half and scoop out the pulp. Mix with the fromage frais.

5. Whip the cream and honey together, then fold carefully into the cheese mixture. Spoon into the biscuit baskets and serve immediately.

Serves 4
Preparation time:
40 minutes
Cooking time:
20 minutes
Freezing:
Recommended for baskets only

MANGO PARFAIT

2 mangoes
juice of 1 lime
125 g (4 oz) caster sugar

2 egg whites
284 ml (10 fl oz) carton
    double cream, whipped

Serves 6
Preparation time:
20 minutes
Freezing time:
About 2 hours

1. Cut the mangoes either side of the stone and scoop out all the flesh. Place in a blender or food processor with the lime juice and 1 tablespoon sugar and work to a purée.
2. Transfer to a rigid freezerproof container, cover, seal and freeze for about 2 hours, until half-frozen.
3. Whisk the egg whites until stiff, then gradually whisk in the remaining sugar.
4. Whisk the half-frozen mango purée, then fold into the meringue mixture, with the cream. Spoon into chilled glasses and serve immediately, with crisp biscuits.

ICED STRAWBERRY BOMBES

1 kg (2 lb) strawberries
1 tablespoon icing sugar
2 tablespoons framboise
    liqueur (optional)
3 egg whites
175 g (6 oz) caster sugar

284 ml (10 fl oz) carton
    double cream, whipped
4 tablespoons smatana or
    single cream
frosted leaves (see page 42)
    to decorate

Serves 10
Preparation time:
40 minutes
Freezing time:
About 3 hours

1. Purée the strawberries in a blender or food processor, then sieve to remove the pips.
2. Place 350 ml (12 fl oz) of the purée in a bowl, stir in the icing sugar, and liqueur if using, and set aside.
3. Whisk the egg whites until stiff, then gradually whisk in the caster sugar until thick. Fold in the cream and remaining strawberry purée.
4. Divide the mixture between ten 150 ml (¼ pint) moulds, cover with foil and freeze for about 3 hours.
5. To serve, dip the moulds into cold water and turn out onto chilled serving plates. Pour a little of the reserved strawberry sauce around each ice.
6. Place the smatana or single cream in a greaseproof paper piping bag, cut off the end and pipe a design on the sauce. Use a skewer to create a marbled effect. Serve immediately, decorated with frosted leaves.

DAMSON ICE CREAM

This looks very pretty served on individual plates, surrounded with the sauce; but if you prefer, serve whole, surrounded with sauce, and slice at the table.

500 g (1 lb) damsons
125 g (4 oz) caster sugar
2 egg whites
50 g (2 oz) icing sugar, sifted

142 ml (5 fl oz) carton double cream, whipped

Serves 8
Preparation time: 40 minutes
Cooking time: 15 minutes
Freezing time: About 3 hours

1. Place the damsons, caster sugar and 4 tablespoons water in a pan, cover and cook gently for 15 minutes, until tender. Cool slightly, remove the stones, then purée in a blender or food processor. Sieve to remove the skins and leave to cool.
2. Whisk the egg whites until stiff, then gradually whisk in the icing sugar. Set aside a quarter of the damson purée, then fold the rest into the egg whites with the cream.
3. Turn into a 1 litre (1¾ pint) mould or 500 g (1 lb) loaf tin, cover with foil and freeze for about 3 hours, until firm.
4. To serve, dip the tin in cold water and turn out. Cut into slices and place on chilled plates.
5. Pour the reserved damson purée around the ice cream slices to serve.

BLACKBERRY AND GERANIUM BOMBE

Sweet-scented geranium leaves give blackberries a wonderful flavour. Of course you can omit them or add 2 tablespoons rosewater instead. This ice cream also looks attractive made in individual freezerproof moulds.

500 g (1 lb) blackberries
3 sweet-scented geranium leaves
4 tablespoons caster sugar
125 ml (4 fl oz) water
50 g (2 oz) granulated sugar
3 egg yolks

450 ml (¾ pint) whipping cream, whipped
TO DECORATE:
6 tablespoons whipped cream
8 blackberries
geranium leaves

1. Put the blackberries, geranium leaves and caster sugar in a pan and simmer for about 10 minutes, until tender. Rub through a sieve and leave to cool.

2. Place the water and granulated sugar in a pan and heat gently, stirring until dissolved. Increase the heat and boil steadily until the syrup reaches 110°C/225°F on a sugar thermometer, or a little of the cooled syrup forms a thread when drawn between thumb and forefinger.

3. Cool slightly, then pour onto the egg yolks, whisking until the mixture is thick and mousse-like.

4. Mix the cream and blackberry purée together, then fold into the egg mixture.

5. Turn into a 1.5 litre (2½ pint) pudding basin and smooth the surface. Cover with foil and freeze for about 5 hours, until firm.

6. To serve, invert the basin onto a serving plate and cover with a cloth wrung out in hot water; give a good shake and the ice cream will come out.

7. Pipe a border of cream around the bottom and leave in the refrigerator for about 30 minutes. Just before serving, decorate with the blackberries and geranium leaves.

Serves 8
Preparation time: 45 minutes
Cooking time: 10 minutes
Freezing time: About 5 hours

LIME ICE CREAM

A refreshing yet very creamy ice cream with a really soft texture, so there is no need to soften before serving.

3 eggs, separated
150 g (5 oz) caster sugar
grated rind and juice of
* 2 limes*

284 ml (10 fl oz) carton
* double cream, whipped*
lime slices to decorate

Serves 8
Preparation time:
20 minutes
Freezing time:
About 3 hours

1. Whisk the egg yolks, half of the sugar and the lime rind together until thick and creamy.
2. Strain the lime juice into a pan, heat gently, then pour onto the egg mixture, whisking until thick.
3. Whisk the egg whites until stiff, then whisk in the remaining sugar. Fold in the lime mixture, with the cream.
4. Turn into a rigid freezerproof container, cover, seal and freeze for about 3 hours, until firm.
5. Scoop into chilled glass dishes and decorate with lime slices to serve.

RASPBERRY CREAM BOMBE

2 eggs, plus 2 yolks
75 g (3 oz) caster sugar
450 ml (¾ pint) single
* cream*
2–3 drops vanilla essence

284 ml (10 fl oz) carton
* double cream, whipped*
½ quantity Raspberry
* Sorbet (page 48),*
* softened*

Serves 8–10
Preparation time:
40 minutes
Freezing time:
About 3½ hours

1. Mix the eggs, egg yolks and sugar together in a bowl.
2. Bring the single cream to the boil, then pour onto the egg mixture, stirring vigorously. Strain, then leave to cool.
3. Add the vanilla essence and fold in the whipped cream.
4. Pour into a rigid freezerproof container, cover, seal and freeze for about 2 hours, until half-frozen. Beat with an electric whisk, cover and return to the freezer for about 30 minutes, until fairly firm.
5. Beat the ice cream to an even consistency, then use to line thickly the inside of a chilled 1.5 litre (2½ pint) bombe mould or pudding basin.
6. Fill the centre with the raspberry sorbet and cover with any remaining ice cream. Put the lid of the bombe mould on, or cover the basin with foil, and freeze for about 1 hour, until firm.
7. To serve, dip the mould or basin into cold water and turn the bombe out onto a chilled serving dish.

KULFI

This is an adaptation of the popular Indian ice cream. In India it is made entirely with milk, which is boiled long enough to reduce the original quantity by a third. Adding the milk powder gives the same result, but takes less time.

600 ml (1 pint) milk
4 tablespoons skimmed
*   milk powder*
seeds from 4 cardamom
*   pods*

4 tablespoons caster sugar
25 g (1 oz) almonds,
*   chopped finely*
25 g (1 oz) pistachio nuts,
*   chopped finely*

Serves 4
Preparation time:
20 minutes
Freezing time:
About 4 hours

1. Whisk the milk and milk powder together, add the cardamom seeds and bring to the boil. Stir in the sugar, then leave until cold.
2. Strain the milk into a rigid freezerproof container, then stir in the almonds and all but 1 tablespoon of the pistachios. Cover, seal and freeze for about 2 hours, until half-frozen.
3. Beat with an electric whisk, cover, seal and return to the freezer for about 2 hours, until firm.
4. Transfer to the refrigerator 30 minutes before serving, to soften. Scoop into chilled glasses and sprinkle with the remaining pistachio nuts to serve.

ICED CHERRY ROULADE

A roulade is always a spectacular and popular dessert. Here I have added cherries to the filling. As the recipe is served iced, it can be prepared well in advance of your dinner party.

150 g (5 oz) plain
*   chocolate, broken into*
*   pieces*
4 eggs, separated
150 g (5 oz) caster sugar
icing sugar for sprinkling
FOR THE FILLING:
1 egg white

50 g (2 oz) icing sugar,
*   sifted*
142 ml (5 fl oz) carton
*   double cream, whipped*
425 g (15 oz) can black
*   cherries, drained, stoned*
*   and chopped*

1. Grease and line a 30 × 20 cm (12 × 8 inch) Swiss roll tin.
2. Place the chocolate and 3 tablespoons water in a pan and heat gently until melted.

3. Whisk the egg yolks with half of the sugar until thick and creamy, then whisk in the warm chocolate.

4. Whisk the egg whites until stiff, then whisk in the remaining sugar. Fold into the chocolate mixture.

5. Turn into the prepared tin. Bake in a preheated oven, 180°C/350°F/Gas Mark 4, for 30–35 minutes, until firm.

6. Leave to cool for 5 minutes, then cover with a clean damp cloth and leave to stand for 3 hours or overnight if more convenient.

7. To make the filling, whisk the egg white until stiff, then whisk in the icing sugar. Fold in the cream and cherries.

8. Carefully remove the cloth from the roulade and turn out onto a sheet of greaseproof paper sprinkled thickly with icing sugar. Peel off the lining paper.

9. Spread the filling over the roulade and roll up like a Swiss roll. Open-freeze for about 3 hours, until firm, then wrap in a polythene bag until required.

10. Sprinkle with icing sugar and cut into slices to serve.

Serves 8
Preparation time:
40 minutes, plus standing time
Cooking time:
30–35 minutes
Freezing time:
About 3 hours

PINEAPPLE SLICE

1 large pineapple
3 egg whites
175 g (6 oz) caster sugar

284 ml (10 fl oz) carton
double cream, whipped

Serves 8
Preparation time:
30 minutes
Freezing time:
About 3 hours

1. Cut the pineapple in half lengthways. Scrape out the flesh and juice, using a fork to loosen the flesh and a spoon to scrape the shells clean. Discard the hard central core and chill the shells. Place the flesh in a blender or food processor and work until smooth.
2. Whisk the egg whites until stiff, then gradually whisk in the sugar. Fold in the cream and pineapple purée.
3. Spoon enough of the mixture into the shells to come to the top and smooth evenly. Cover with foil and freeze for about 3 hours, until firm. Place the remaining mixture in a rigid container, cover, seal and freeze.
4. To serve, cut each pineapple half into 4 slices and place on chilled individual plates. Scoop the remaining ice cream into balls and arrange next to each slice.

COCONUT CREAM ICE

50 g (2 oz) creamed
*   coconut, blended with*
*   3 tablespoons boiling*
*   water*
2 eggs, separated
125 g (4 oz) caster sugar
284 ml (10 fl oz) carton
*   single cream*

142 ml (5 fl oz) carton
*   double cream, whipped*
150 ml (¼ pint) Chocolate
*   Sauce**
4 tablespoons smatana or
*   single cream*

Serves 8
Preparation time:
20 minutes
Freezing time:
About 3 hours

1. Place the blended coconut, egg yolks and half of the sugar in a bowl and beat well.
2. Bring the single cream to the boil, then pour onto the egg mixture, stirring vigorously. Return to the pan and cook gently until thickened slightly. Leave to cool.
3. Whisk the egg whites until stiff, then whisk in the remaining sugar. Fold in the cream and coconut custard.
4. Turn into a rigid freezerproof container, cover, seal and freeze for about 3 hours, until firm.
5. Transfer to the refrigerator 20 minutes before serving, to soften. Scoop onto individual serving plates and pour round the chocolate sauce.
6. Fill a greaseproof paper piping bag with the smatana or cream, cut off the end and pipe a design on the sauce.

ICED PASSION FRUIT SOUFFLÉS

Serve as soon as you have removed the foil, or the raised
ice cream will begin to drip.

8 ripe passion fruit
1 teaspoon lemon juice
2 eggs, separated
125 g (4 oz) caster sugar

284 ml (10 fl oz) carton
double cream, whipped
25–50 g (1–2 oz) pistachio
nuts, chopped

Serves 6
Preparation time:
35 minutes
Freezing time:
About 3 hours

1. Tie double bands of foil around the outside of 6 small
freezerproof ramekins, to stand 2.5 cm (1 inch) above the
rims.
2. Cut the passion fruit in half and scoop the pulp into a
sieve over a bowl. Press through the sieve to extract as
much juice as possible; discard the seeds. Stir in the lemon
juice.
3. Place the egg yolks and half of the sugar in a bowl and
beat with an electric whisk until thick and mousse-like.
4. Whisk the egg whites until stiff, then whisk in the
remaining sugar. Fold into the egg yolk mixture with the
passion fruit juice and the cream.
5. Spoon into the prepared ramekins, place on a baking
sheet and open freeze for about 3 hours, until firm.
6. Remove the foil carefully and sprinkle the pistachio
nuts over each soufflé to serve.

ICED RASPBERRY SPONGE

A cinnamon-flavoured sponge that encloses a frozen raspberry filling. Melba sauce completes this simple yet impressive dessert.

2 eggs
75 g (3 oz) caster sugar
50 g (2 oz) plain flour
1 teaspoon ground
cinnamon
FOR THE FILLING:
250 g (8 oz) raspberries
2 egg whites

125 g (4 oz) caster sugar
142 ml (5 fl oz) carton
double cream, whipped
TO FINISH:
150 ml (1/4 pint) Melba
Sauce*
frosted raspberry leaves
(see page 42)

1. Grease and line an 18 cm (7 inch) square cake tin.
2. Place the eggs and sugar in a bowl and beat with an
electric whisk, until thick and mousse-like.

3. Sift the flour and cinnamon together, then carefully fold into the whisked mixture.

4. Turn into the prepared tin and bake in a preheated oven, 190°C/375°F/Gas Mark 5, for 25–30 minutes, until the cake springs back when lightly pressed. Cool on a wire rack.

5. To make the filling, rub the raspberries through a nylon sieve to remove the pips.

6. Whisk the egg whites until stiff peaks form, then gradually whisk in the sugar. Fold in the raspberry purée and the cream.

7. Split the cake in half horizontally. Place the bottom half in the cleaned cake tin. Spoon the filling over the top, spreading evenly to the edges. Cover with the remaining sponge, pressing gently together. Cover with foil and freeze for about 3 hours, until firm.

8. To serve, dip the tin in cold water to loosen the cake and turn out. Cut in half lengthways, then into slices. Place on chilled plates, pour over the melba sauce and decorate with the frosted leaves.

Serves 8
Preparation time:
45 minutes
Cooking time:
25–30 minutes
Freezing time:
About 3 hours

SAUCES

CHOCOLATE SAUCE

Serve with vanilla, chocolate or coffee ice cream.

175 g (6 oz) plain chocolate, broken into pieces
150 ml (1/4 pint) water

1 teaspoon instant coffee granules
50 g (2 oz) dark brown soft sugar

Makes 300 ml (1/2 pint)
Preparation time: 8 minutes
Freezing: Recommended

1. Place all the ingredients in a small pan and heat gently until melted.
2. Stir thoroughly, then simmer gently for about 3 minutes. Serve warm or cold.

MELBA SAUCE

Serve with raspberry or vanilla ice cream.

350 g (12 oz) raspberries   *4 tablespoons clear honey*

Makes 250 ml (8 fl oz)
Preparation time: 10 minutes
Freezing: Recommended

Place the raspberries and honey in a blender or food processor and work until smooth. Rub through a nylon sieve to remove the pips.

STRAWBERRY SAUCE

Serve with strawberry or vanilla ice cream.

250 g (8 oz) strawberries
1 tablespoon icing sugar, sifted

2 tablespoons framboise liqueur or Cointreau

Makes 150 ml (1/4 pint)
Preparation time: 10 minutes
Freezing: Recommended

1. Place the strawberries and icing sugar in a food processor or blender and work until smooth. Rub through a nylon sieve to remove the pips.
2. Stir in the liqueur.

MANGO SAUCE

For a special dessert, add 2 tablespoons Cointreau or other orange-flavoured liqueur. This sauce is delicious with vanilla ice cream.

1 mango   *150 ml (¼ pint) pure*
                          orange juice

1. Cut the mango either side of the stone and scoop out all the flesh, discarding the stone.
2. Place the flesh in a food processor or blender with the orange juice and work until smooth.
3. Serve warm or cold.

Makes about
300 ml (½ pint)
Preparation time:
10 minutes
Freezing:
Recommended

CRÉMETS

Serve with fresh fruit or fruit compotes.

6 tablespoons double   *2 teaspoons clear honey*
*   cream, whipped*   *   (optional)*
125 g (4 oz) natural
*   fromage frais*

Fold the cream into the fromage frais, sweetening with the honey if you wish. Turn into a shallow dish and chill until required.

Makes 250 ml
(8 fl oz)
Preparation time:
10 minutes
Freezing:
Recommended

REDCURRANT SAUCE

A fresh, sharp-tasting sauce, ideal to serve with rich, creamy or cake-based desserts.

175 g (6 oz) redcurrants   *1 tablespoon clear honey*

1. Rub 125 g (4 oz) of the redcurrants through a nylon sieve into a bowl.
2. Stir the honey into the redcurrant purée, then stir in the remaining redcurrants.

Makes 150 ml
(¼ pint)
Preparation time:
10 minutes
Freezing:
Recommended

INDEX

Photography by: Charlie Stebbings
Designed by: Sue Storey
Home economist: Carole Handslip
Stylist: Antonia Gaunt
Illustration by: Linda Smith
Typeset by Rowland Phototypesetting Limited